Cowee Sam's Family Fun
Cookbook

Cowee Sam Series
Suminski Family Books

by Claire Suminski
and Susan Swedlund

We would like to thank all of our family, friends and readers that contributed recipes and ideas to this cookbook. We would also like to acknowledge our Illustrator, Ros Webb, for the use of her beautiful watercolor paintings from the Cowee Sam series. Special thanks go out to Jacqueline Bourne of OK B Healthy for her wonderful contributions and also to the spectacular staff at Suminski Family Books. Your dedication and hard work is much appreciated.

Our gratitude extends to Joe Suminski and Glen Swedlund who support and encourage us in all our endeavors.

Most of all, we are thankful to our heavenly Father for His grace and love.

Claire Suminski and Susan Swedlund
May 12, 2019

First Edition
ISBN 978-1-7320639-5-2

Library of Congress Control Number (LCCN): 2019936794

Published by Red Press Co.

Redpressco.com

Table of Contents

Introduction and Kitchen Basics

Section 1: Recipes from our Suminski Family Books

Recipe Key

- Main Dish Recipe
- Side Dish/Specialty Recipe
- Dessert Recipe

Section 2: Illustrated Recipes

Section 3: From Farm to Table

More Cooking Tips for Families

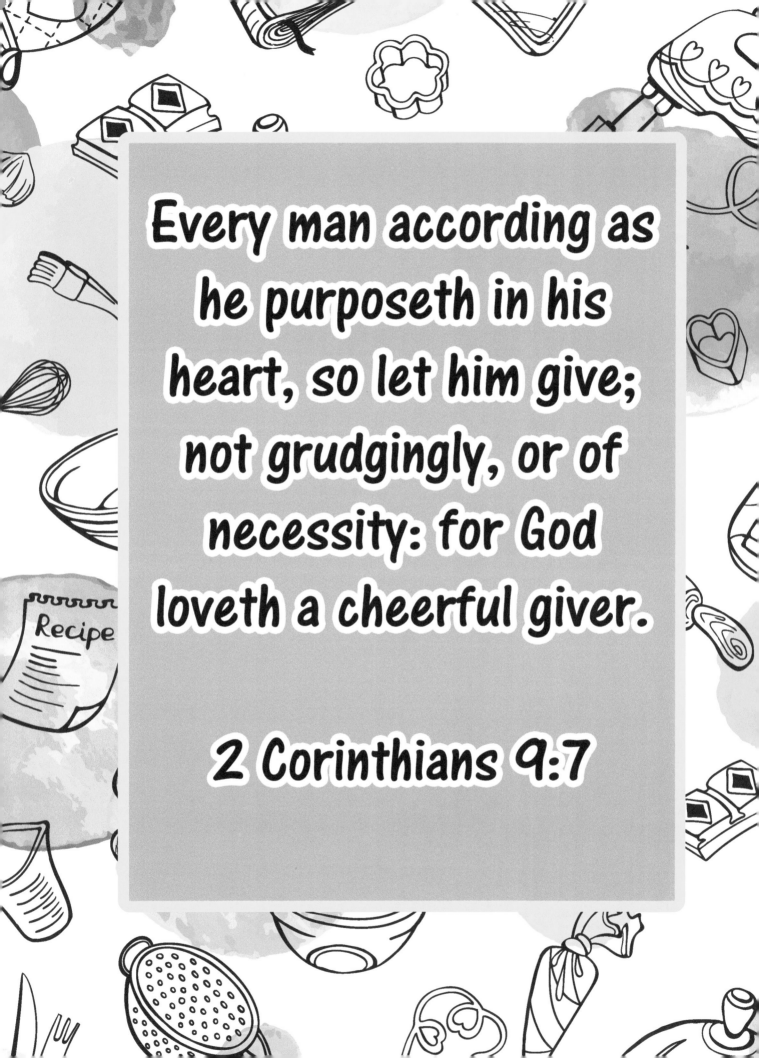

Every man according as he purposeth in his heart, so let him give; not grudgingly, or of necessity: for God loveth a cheerful giver.

2 Corinthians 9:7

Introduction

Food nourishes our bodies and helps us to grow strong and stay healthy. When the food tastes great and people are enjoying themselves, it is truly a sweet gathering. Cooking for others is a great way to show them love and kindness. It is also a great way to show hospitality. Being hospitable simply means to show care, by being lovingly and cheerfully attentive. An example of this would be taking good care of others when they are in your home by making sure they have something good to eat and drink. God encourages us to love and to be hospitable. Learning to cook is fun and a great way to give and serve one another.

> **1 John 4:11**
> Beloved, if God so loved us, we ought also to love one another.

> **Romans 12:13**
> Distributing to the necessity of saints; given to hospitality.

Working and learning as a family is also a sweet time to be together. We hope this book helps you grow in your cooking abilities and also provides great family memories as you learn new skills in the kitchen.

Love,
Claire and Susan

Whenever you see this symbol in one of our recipes, it means an adult should be assisting you to help keep you safe in the kitchen.

Adult Supervision needed

5 IMPORTANT THINGS TO REMEMBER WHEN WORKING IN THE KITCHEN:

1. WASH YOUR HANDS

First wash your hands with soap and water and then as needed throughout your cooking time. It is best not to lick your fingers or touch your face while working in the kitchen. If you forget, wash your hands again.

2

2. CLEAN AS YOU GO.

If something spills, stop and clean it up. When you are through using an item (bowl, knives or other items), rinse and then wash in warm, sudsy water. This helps stop the spread of germs and makes your cooking environment more enjoyable.

3. KNIFE SAFETY

Place your cutting surface slightly above the height of your waist and always wear closed-toe shoes while using sharp knives. If you need to stand on a stool or chair to be at the correct height, make sure it is very stable. Bend your fingers to make a claw (see picture) with the hand that is holding your food, or use a knife guard. This will help protect your fingers.

"THE CLAW"

For young children, begin with slicing a banana with a plastic knife in order to gain confidence and practice good hand positioning.

Also, when cutting anything round, start by cutting it in half, so that you can place the flat surface down. That will make it easier and much safer to cut. When you are through using your knife, give it to your supervising adult to wash it, dry it and put it away. Never put knives in the dish water to soak (It is hard to see in the water and someone may get cut reaching in to the water).

4. CHECK BEFORE YOU TASTE

It is important to check the flavor of your dish to see if the seasonings are to your liking. Some foods, like raw eggs or meat, may not be safe to taste until they are fully cooked. Check with the adult helping you in order to make sure it is safe. After you use a spoon to taste your dish, put it in the sink to wash. If you need to taste again later, use a clean spoon.

5. BE AWARE OF HEAT

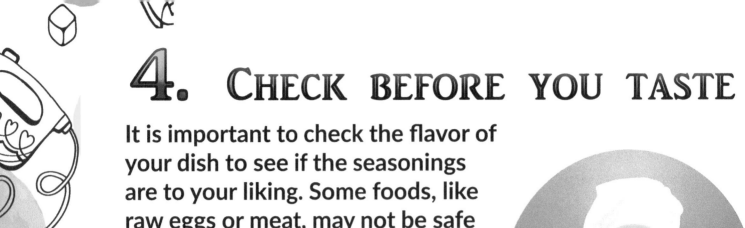

Adult Supervision needed

Be aware of hot surfaces. Do not ever touch a stove top to see whether it is hot. Turn pot handles to the side and make sure to use pot holders when touching the handles. For dishes like pasta, where boiling water is involved, ask an adult to assist you.

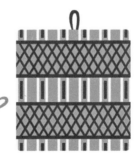

This chart will come in very handy as you are learning new recipes. For instance, a recipe may call for a ¼ cup of butter (on the side of most sticks of butter there are marks indicating Tablespoons). Using this chart you will know that 4 Tablespoons=¼ cup.

KITCHEN MEASUREMENT UNIT CONVERSION

1 TEASPOON (TSP) = 5ML

1 TABLESPOON (TBSP) = 3 TEASPOONS = 15ML

2 TABLESPOONS = 1 OZ (1 FLUID OUNCE) = 30ML

4 TABLESPOONS = 1/4 CUP = 60ML

5 TABLESPOONS + 1 TEASPOONS = 1/3 CUP = 80ML

1/2 CUP = 8 TABLESPOONS = 120ML

1 CUP = 16 TABLESPOONS = 240ML

1 QUART = 2 PINTS = 4 CUPS

1 GALLON = 4 QUARTS = 16 CUPS

FOOD PRESENTATION

All of our senses help us experience eating, especially the sense of sight. When food is presented with love and care, this can help people experience food flavors more intensely. There are simple ways to add beauty to your plates.

HAVE VARIETY IN COLOR AND TEXTURES

ADD GARNISHES

Garnishes are little additions to your plate or serving platter that brighten up and decorate. They add a finishing touch that beautifies your food. The most commonly used garnishes are parsley, parmesan cheese, and lemon slices. You can find a tutorial in the back of this book for these other fun garnishes.

Carrot Curls

Lemon Twists

Radish Fans

Kitchen Utensils

Bowls

Knives

Mixer

Pots

Measuring Spoons

Ladle

Spoon

Whisk

Pans

Measuring Cups

Casserole Dish with Cover

Spatulas

Pot Holders

Grater

Cutting Board

It is important to learn the names of the tools you are using in the kitchen. It will help you understand the steps in recipes and help you communicate with cooking partners more effectively.

Recipes from our Suminski Family Books

SECTION ONE

Cowee Mountain Valley Farm Sunrise Casserole

This is a great way to use up odds and ends in your refrigerator, along with some fresh picked vegetables. It can be different every time!

Ingredients:

18 eggs
1-2 cups of pre-cooked meat of your choice cut into small cubes
        (sausage, ham, turkey, or chicken)
1-2 cups of any in season vegetables cut up
2-3 cups of cubed bread slices (stale or dryed out bread work the best)
1 cup of grated cheese
½ teaspoon of salt
¼ teaspoon of pepper
1 teaspoon dried herb of choice or 1 Tablespoon fresh herb
        (basil, oregano, thyme)

Directions:

1. Preheat oven to 350 degrees. In a large bowl crack and beat your eggs, then add the remaining ingredients except the cheese.
2. Pour this mixture into a greased casserole dish and sprinkle the cheese on top.
3. Cover with tin foil.
4. Bake in a 350 degree oven for 50-70 minutes (depending on the size of your casserole dish)
5. Cool for ten minutes then cut into squares and serve. This will serve approximately 8-10 people.

Adult Supervision needed

Cowee Sam

"Early the next morning, as Farmer Joe's wife put her family's favorite egg casserole into the oven, Sam started urgently barking, "Ruff, Ruff, Ruff!"

page 32

9

Aunt Molly's Famous Blueberry Pie

Ingredients:

Mema's Flakey Vinegar Pie Crust:

3 cups of flour
1½ cups of shortening, lard, or butter
Pinch of salt
5 Tablespoons of water
1 egg
1 Tablespoon of apple cider vinegar
1 teaspoon of sugar + 1 egg white (for final step before baking)

Blueberry Filling:

6 cups of blueberries
¾ cup of sugar
1 teaspoon of lemon zest
2 teaspoons of lemon juice
Pinch of fresh ground nutmeg
3-4 Tablespoons of Minute Tapioca
    (best if ground up in grinder or food processor)

Swiftwater Rescue

I'll tell you more when I get home. Annie, is there pie in the oven?"
"Yes, Grandpa, and it smells great. Yours are in the oven now, and we are just finishing up the ones to bring to the emergency shelter."

Directions:
1. Preheat oven to 350 degrees and then in a large bowl cut in (with two knives, a pastry cutter, or your fingers) the flour, the shortening, lard, or butter, and a pinch of salt.
2. In a small bowl, beat in 5 Tablespoons of water and 1 egg. Mix well then add 1 Tablespoon of apple cider vinegar.
3. Add vinegar blend to the flour mixture and mix.
4. Form into two balls and then roll them out onto wax paper.
5. Place one into your pie tin and save the other to make the top crust.
6. In a large bowl combine all the blueberry filling ingredients and mix gently together.
7. Add blueberry mixture to the dough-lined pie plate.
8. With remaining crust make a lattice top crust (see photos on the next page), trim and crimp the edges.
9. Brush the top crust with egg white and sprinkle with sugar.
10. Bake at 400 degrees for 15 minutes and then reduce to 350 degrees for 45 minutes.

Making Aunt Molly's Famous Blueberry Pie

Make crust according to the recipe on pages 10 and 11 of this book and form into two balls. Take the first ball and place it on a floured surface.

Roll out dough evenly into a circular shape.

Cover the dough in plastic wrap and roll the dough to transfer it into the pie plate.

Transfer to pie plate and take off the plastic wrap.

Adjust the crust and press into plate

Brush the crust with egg whites

Gather the filling ingredients listed in the recipe on page 10.

Mix the pie filling ingredients together.

Put the filling into the pie crust.

Roll out the second ball of dough to form the top crust.

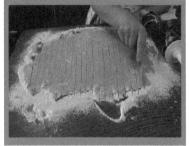

Cut the dough into even strips about 1 inch thick.

Lay the strips horizontally

Weave in the vertical strips to make a beautiful lattice crust

Crimp the edges by pressing the dough hanging over onto the rim of the pie plate.

You can use any left over dough to make a decoration on top.

THis pie is super delicious and really FUN to make and share!

15 minutes

45 minutes

Bake at 400 degrees for 15 minutes
Then
Bake at 350 degrees for 45 minutes

Let cool then ENJOY!

13

Celebration Hot Chocolate

Ingredients: (Serves 6)
⅓ cup of sugar
6 Tablespoons of unsweetened cocoa powder
6 Tablespoons of water
6 cups of milk
½ teaspoon of vanilla extract
½ teaspoon of cinnamon

Directions:

1. Combine sugar, cocoa, and water in small saucepan. Bring to boil over medium heat, stirring constantly.
2. Add milk and heat until steaming. Do not boil.
3. Add vanilla and cinnamon.
4. Serve in mugs, and if desired, top with whipped cream or marshmallows.
5. Drink with friends and family, rejoicing and celebrating with thankful hearts.

With God's help we did it Sam!

Adult Supervision required

Swift Water Rescue

"A few minutes later, they are all snuggled in front of the fire and giving thanks to God for the rescue."

page 31

14

Solar Eclipse Cookies

Ingredients:

¾ cup of butter
2 cups of sugar
2 eggs
½ cup molasses
2 teaspoons of vinegar
3 ¾ cups of plain flour
1½ teaspoons of baking soda
2-3 teaspoons ginger
½ teaspoon of cinnamon
¼ teaspoon cloves
Marshmallows

Directions:

1. Preheat oven to 325 degrees. Cream butter and sugar, add eggs, molasses and vinegar.

2. Sift dry ingredients and add to creamed mixture.

3. Form into ¾ inch balls and bake on parchment paper lined cookie sheet for 10 minutes.

4. Cut marshmallow in half and put cut side down on almost baked cookies. Return to the oven for about 2 minutes.

Solar Eclipse

"Ruby marveled at the photos and handed Annie a cup of tea and a plate of delicious Solar Eclipse cookies that they had made earlier in the day." *page 14*

15

Grandma Ruby's Shortbread

Ingredients
2 cups salted butter, softened
1 cup packed brown sugar
4 to 4½ cups all-purpose flour

1. Preheat the oven to 325 degrees.
2. Cream the butter and brown sugar until light and fluffy.
3. Add 3 and ¾ cups of flour; mix well.
4. Turn dough onto a floured surface; knead for five minutes, adding enough remaining flour to form a soft dough.
5. Roll to ½ inch thickness. Cut into 3 x 1 inch strips.
6. Place 1 inch apart on an ungreased baking sheet. Chill for a few minutes in the refrigerator and then prick with a fork.
7. Bake until cookies are lightly browned, 20 to 25 minutes. The key is to watch shortbread closely, and when it is just turning golden brown, remove from the oven. Then let them cool.

Scottish Highlands Games Adventure

After Brenda and Ruby finished getting ready for the day, they headed for the Scottish Baking Contest tent to register Ruby's shortbread. Ruby only used the best ingredients in her shortbread. It was buttery and crisp.

17

Page 15

Shepherd's Pie

Ingredients:
1 ½ - 2 pounds potatoes (about 3 large) peeled and quartered
8 tablespoons butter (1 stick)
1 medium onion, chopped (about 1½ cups)
1-2 cups vegetables – diced carrots, corn, peas
1 lbs ground beef
½ lbs of ground pork sausage
½ cup beef broth
1 teaspoon of Worcestershire sauce
Salt, pepper, other seasonings of choice

Scottish Highlands Games Adventure

"Many of the members of Clan Bruce had brought authentic Scottish foods to share with each other."

Page 7

Directions:

Adult Supervision needed

1. Place the potatoes in a medium pot and cover with an inch of cold water, add a teaspoon of salt. Bring to a boil, reduce to simmer, cook until tender (about 20 minutes).

2. Sautee the vegetables: melt 4 Tablespoons of the butter in a large sauce pan on medium heat. Add the chopped onions and cook until tender (about 6-10 minutes).

Tip: Add vegetables according to their cooking time. For instance, carrots should be cooked with the onions because they take as long to cook as the onions do.
If you are including peas or corn, add them toward the end of the cooking of the onions, or after the meat starts to cook, as they take very little cooking time.

3. Add the ground beef and sausage to the pan with the onions and vegetables. Cook until no longer pink. Season with salt and pepper.

4. Add the Worcestershire sauce and beef broth. Bring the broth to a simmer and reduce heat to low. Cook uncovered for ten minutes, adding more beef broth if necessary to keep the meat from drying out.

5. Mash the cooked potatoes: When the potatoes are done cooking, remove them from the pot and place them in a bowl with the remaining 4 Tablespoons of butter. Mash with a fork and season with salt and pepper.

6. Preheat oven to 400 degrees.

7. Spread the beef, onions, and vegetables in an even layer in a large baking dish (9x13 works well).

8. Spread the mashed potatoes over the top of the ground beef. Rough up the surface of the mashed potatoes with a fork so there are peaks that will get well browned.

9. Cook in oven until browned and bubbling (about 30 minutes) . If necessary, broil for the last few minutes to help the surface of the mashed potatoes brown.

Jerome's Favorite Baked Scotch Eggs

Ingredients

1lb ground pork sausage
1 teaspoon dried minced onion
1 teaspoon salt
4 hard-cooked eggs, peeled
All-purpose flour, as needed
¾ cup panko crispy bread crumbs
1 egg

1. Preheat oven to 400 degrees. In large bowl, mix pork sausage, onion and salt. Shape mixture into 4 equal patties.
2. Roll each hard-cooked egg in flour to coat; place on sausage patty and shape sausage around egg. Dip each into beaten egg; coat with bread crumbs to cover completely. Place on ungreased cookie sheet.
3. Bake 35 minutes or until sausage is thoroughly cooked and no longer pink near egg. Slice Scotch eggs in half and serve.

Scottish Highlands Games Adventure

"Ruby brought Scotch eggs and scones from home, too! None of their party would go hungry this morning! "   page 11

Mema's Irish Stew

Ingredients:

½ cup of flour (gluten-free option: almond flour)
½ teaspoon of salt
¼ teaspoon of pepper
2 Tablespoons of oil
1-1½ pounds of lamb cut up into large cubes
2 cups of vegetable or beef stock
4 carrots cut into 1-inch chunks
3 celery stalks cut into ½- inch chunks
2 medium onions cut into small chunks
4 small/medium potatoes cut into large chunks
1 small head of cabbage cut into medium pieces
Splash of Guinness Ale (optional)

Mema

"Mema was a good cook too, and showed us how to make Irish Stew."

page 25

Directions:

1. Combine ½ cup of flour, ½ teaspoon of salt, and ¼ teaspoon of pepper, in a bowl and mix together.

2. Roll chunks of lamb into the seasoned flour mixture, coating well.

3. Heat 2 Tablespoons of oil in a cast iron skillet. Sear the chunks of lamb on both sides and then pour into crockpot and add 2 cups of vegetable or beef stock to it.

4. Deglaze the bottom of the skillet with a cup of water and add that to the crockpot.

5. Add the carrots, celery, and onions to the meat and broth mixture. If desired, also add a splash of Guinness Ale at this time.

6. Cook on High, in the crockpot, for 3 hours, stirring occasionally, then add the chunks of potatoes and cabbage, also add a sprig of rosemary. Cook on High for an additional 3 hours.

7. Before serving, take out the sprig of rosemary and then salt and pepper to taste.

Irish Soda Bread

AUTHENTIC IRISH CUISINE

Ingredients:
3 cups of flour
½ teaspoon of baking soda
1 teaspoon of salt
2 Tablespoons of sugar
½ cup of dried currants
1 egg
1¼ cup buttermilk
4 Tablespoons of butter

Mema

"The potatoes we dug from the garden were very delicious in the stew. The Irish Soda Bread we made was just right with the stew and soaked up the gravy."

page 25

Directions:
1. Preheat oven to 400 degrees. Lightly grease a large baking sheet or line it with parchment paper. Soak currants in ½ cup of buttermilk for 20 minutes.
2. In large bowl, mix together flour, baking soda, sugar, and salt. Make a well in the center, add the egg, ½ cup of buttermilk, and 2 Tablespoons of melted butter, then stir together.
3. Add the currants with the buttermilk they were soaking in, and mix until well incorporated (if the mixture seems too dry add ⅛ cup of buttermilk and re-mix).
4. Turn the dough out onto a floured surface and knead slightly. Form the dough into a round shape and place on the prepared baking sheet.
5. In a small bowl, add the remaining 2 Tablespoons of melted butter to ⅛ cup of buttermilk and brush the loaf with this mixture.
6. Bake in preheated oven until a toothpick inserted in the center of the loaf comes out clean. This should be around 40-50 minutes. The bottom of the bread will have a hollow sound when tapped, and this will help you know when it is done.

Carrot Oat Applesauce Treats for Dogs and Horses

Ingredients:

½ cup oats

(Quick oats for dogs, steel cut, quick/instant or old fashioned for horses)

½ cup unsweetened applesauce
½ cup (about 1 large) grated carrot
½ cup all-purpose flour

Directions:

1. Preheat the oven to 350 degrees and cover a baking tray with parchment paper or a silicone baking mat.
2. Mix all four ingredients in a medium bowl.
3. Use a tablespoon to drop clumps of the mixture on to the baking tray. If desired make into shapes (Quick/Instant oats do not shape well).
4. Bake for 18-20 minutes, until treats are set.

Adult Supervision Needed

Recipe Notes:
These keep in the fridge for 5-7 days.

Rides Again!

"Annie gave them each some of the treats she had made that morning, and they wolfed them right down."

page 29

26

Design your own Soup!

Most people enjoy a good soup! They are easy and fun to make, and are a good way to develop your seasoning skills. So grab a pot, get adventurous, and let's make some tasty, scrumptious soup!

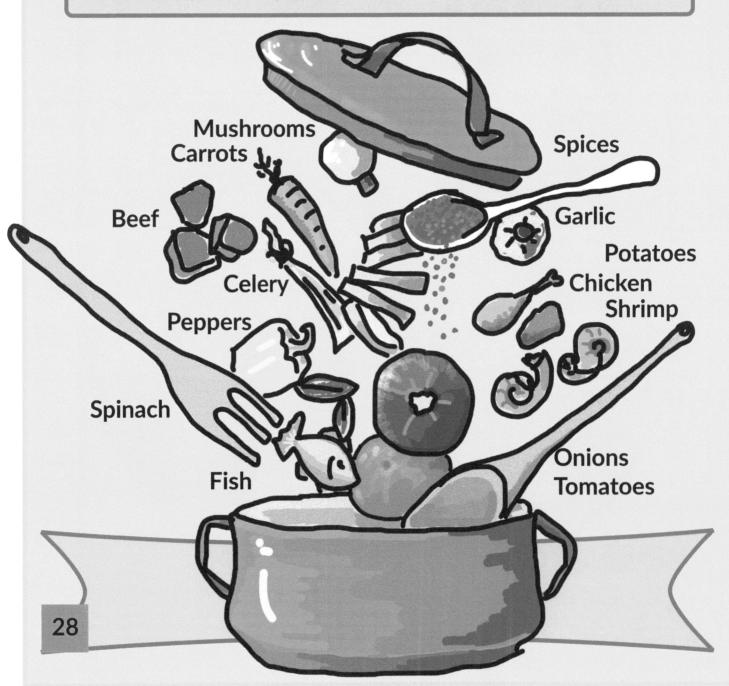

Mushrooms
Carrots
Spices
Beef
Garlic
Potatoes
Celery
Chicken
Shrimp
Peppers
Spinach
Onions
Tomatoes
Fish

1. CHOOSE A BASE:

Here are some options-

<u>Vegetable base</u>: In a medium pot throw in some root vegetables such as carrots, onions, potatoes, parsnips or turnips. Celery is also a great addition. Add water to cover the vegetables and bring to a boil, then simmer on low for about twenty minutes, or until the vegetables are soft. With a slotted spoon carefully remove the vegetables and puree them in a food processor, then return them to the pot and mix with the remaining water. You now have a delicious base to add your other ingredients.

<u>Chicken, Beef, or Fish Stock</u>: If you want, you could add milk or cream to the stock; it is up to you.

<u>Tomato puree</u>: This can be used on its own or can be added to the stock or vegetable base.

2. IF DESIRED, CHOOSE A MEAT:

Chicken, turkey, ground beef, steak, fish, shrimp, pork sausage or kielbasa. Keep in mind the base you have chosen. A chicken stock goes well with just about any of these, but a fish stock would be better with fish or shrimp and beef stock with ground beef, steak, or sausage.

29

3. CHOOSE YOUR OTHER ADD-INS:

Vegetables in cubes, chunks, or slices: Onions, garlic, carrots, potatoes,mushrooms, and celery are the most common.

Rice, Pasta, or Beans, Spinach or Kale

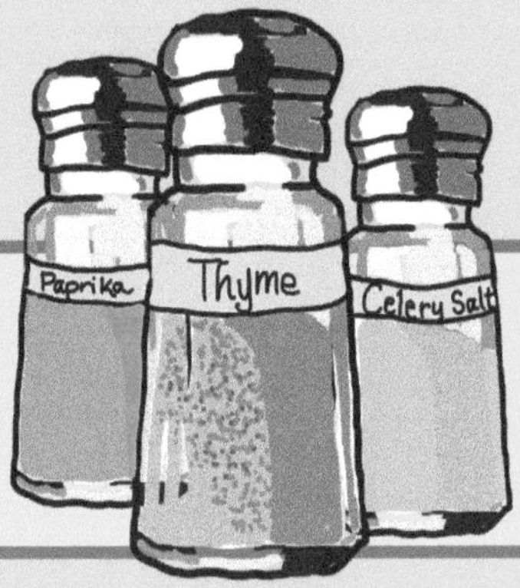

4. CHOOSE YOUR SPICES:

Add salt and pepper and other flavors that go with your chosen base or meat. After adding your spices, bring to a boil and let simmer for 20 minutes. The following chart may be helpful, but the possibilities are endless!

CHICKEN	Celery seed, marjoram, thyme, parsley, basil, and sage
BEEF	Marjoram, rosemary, thyme
FISH/SHRIMP	Oregano, thyme, bay leaf, paprika, and celery salt
TOMATO BASED	Basil, oregano, or fennel
CREAM BASED	Parsley or thyme

Aunt Sophie's Dumplings

1 ½ cups of flour,
4 Tablespoons of butter,
4 eggs

Adult Supervision needed

Directions:

1. Boil 8-10 cups of water.
2. Beat eggs in a bowl, then add the flour and mix well.
3. Stir the water with a spoon to make the spoon hot. This will make the batter fall off the spoon easier.
4. Drop the batter by spoonfuls into the boiling water, stirring ocasionally during the process.
5. Lower the temperature of the water and cook the dumplings until done, 15-18 minutes.
6. Drain the water and take out the dumplings. Then add butter to the pot, stir in the dumplings and add salt and pepper to taste. Makes 2-3 servings.

You can add this to your soup, just using smaller spoonfuls. Cook as directed, then add to your soup. This eliminates the need for butter in step 6.

Make your own Mayonnaise

Ingredients:
1 cup of avacado oil
1 large egg
1 teaspoon of lemon juice
1/2 teaspoon of dijon mustard
1/4 teaspoon of salt

This is a fun recipe to experiment with, adding different flavors and seasonings!

Directions:
1. Add all ingredients to a 16 oz. Mason Jar (or any other jar of similar size and shape).
2. Blend from the bottom for 20-30 seconds, then slowly raise the blender up and down until the mixture has thickened to the desired consistency.
3. Do a taste test, and then you may want to add more salt or lemon juice. If you do so, blend for another 20-30 seconds.
4. Keep this stored for up to two weeks in the refrigerator.

Grow your Own
Pizza Herb Garden in a Pot

Roma Tomato Plant

Oregano

Basil

Basil

Parsley

Recipes using your Pizza Herb Garden on pages 34-37

Herbs are easy and fun to grow! In a large pot, place in the middle 1 Roma tomato plant, then surround it with basil, oregano and parsley.

Upside Down Pizza Casserole

Gluten Free

Ingredients:

Filling:

1 pound of Italian sausage (pork or turkey)

1- 8oz. can of tomato sauce

1- 6 oz. can of tomato paste

½ cup of red onion diced

½ cup of green pepper diced

1 clove of garlic or ¼ teaspoon of garlic powder

2 cups of fresh spinach

2 Roma tomatoes diced

4 teaspoons of fresh basil or 2 teaspoons dried

6 teaspoons of fresh oregano or 2 teaspoons dried

2 teaspoons of fresh parsley or 1 teaspoon dried

Upper Crust:

1 cup of almond flour

1 teaspoon of baking powder

1 cup of shredded cheddar cheese

½ cup of shredded mozzarella cheese

¼ teaspoon of pepper

4 eggs

2 Tablespoons of cream

1. Over medium heat cook sausage in a cast iron frying pan, crumble with a wooden spoon as it cooks.

Adult Supervision needed

2. When the sausage is cooked, add in the red onion, bell pepper, minced garlic, and spinach. Sauté the vegetables until they start to soften, then add in the basil, oregano, parsley.

3. Stir in the tomato sauce and the tomato paste and mix well. Add in a ¼ cup of water and let simmer about 5 minutes, then add in the Roma tomatoes. Let simmer for an additional 5 minutes.

PLAY AROUND WITH DIFFERENT FILLINGS AND MAKE YOUR OWN VERSION OF THIS RECIPE!
EXAMPLE: INSTEAD OF SAUSAGE, ADD CHICKEN AND MUSHROOMS, AND INSTEAD OF 8 OZ. TOMATO SAUCE, ADD 8 OZ. OF HEAVY WHIPPING CREAM, AND INSTEAD OF 6 OZ. OF TOMATO PASTE ADD 6 OZ. CREAM CHEESE.

4. Preheat oven to 400 degrees. Mix the ingredients for the upper crust in a medium size bowl.

5. Spread the crust dough over the meat mixture and bake at 400 degrees for 12-18 minutes, or until the crust is golden brown.

Adult Supervision needed

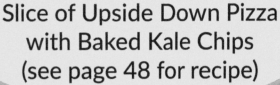
Slice of Upside Down Pizza with Baked Kale Chips (see page 48 for recipe)

CRUST SUBSTITUTIONS:

YOU CAN EASILY REPLACE THE CRUST IN THIS RECIPE WITH FROZEN PREMADE PIE CRUST OR USE A BISQUICK TYPE OF MIX INSTEAD.

Easy Breezy Pizza Toast

Ingredients:
1 piece of toasted bread of choice
Ketchup or Homemade Pizza Sauce *(pg.38)
2 leaves of fresh basil or small pinch of dried
1 leaf of oregano and parsley or small sprinkle of dried
4 pieces of pepperoni, cooked sausage or vegetables
Mozzarella Cheese slice or shredded

*If using the Organic Pizza Sauce recipe on page 38, then leave out the Oregano.

Try using an English Muffin or French Bread in place of the toast

Lay or sprinkle Mozzeralla on top of the sauce

Sprinkle on herbs

Spread Ketchup/Sauce onto toasted bread

Lastly, add Pepperoni, sausage or vegetables

Adult Supervision needed

Broil in Toaster Oven or Microwave until the cheese is melted and enjoy!

OK B Healthy's
Organic Pizza Sauce

Directions:

1. Place desired amount of Organic Tomato Sauce (Hunts and Muir Glen carry sugar free options) on pizza crust or toasted bread (see recipe on page 37).
2. Then sprinkle the sauce lightly with salt and organic seasonings: garlic powder, onion powder, and oregano.

As easy as that you have sugar free, organic Pizza Sauce!

For more OKbHealthy recipes visit:
https://www.facebook.com/okbhealthy

Peanut Butter Cookies

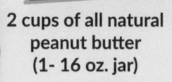

1

2 cups of all natural
peanut butter
(1- 16 oz. jar)

1 cup of sugar
or sugar replacement of choice
(such as Swerve)

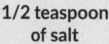

1 teaspoon
of both
baking powder
and vanilla
extract

1/2 teaspoon
of salt

2

2 eggs

MIX WELL

3

Preheat oven to 350 degrees. Form batter into 1 ½ inch balls
and place onto a baking sheet lined with parchment paper.
Press down each ball with a fork. Bake for 9 to 10 minutes.
Let cool on baking rack until firm. Store in refrigerator.

Maple Press Cookies

Another healthy recipe from
OK B Healthy

Organic Ingredients:
2 cups of firmly packed almond flour
½ cup of maple syrup
A pinch of Pink Himalayan sea salt
You will also need:
1 small Mason Jar
1 dish of water

Directions:

1. Preheat the oven to 350 degrees and mix the almond flour, maple syrup, and the salt in a bowl and gently mix. If the mix seems too dry, add a touch more maple syrup.

2. Take a spoonful and roll into a ball using your hands. Place on a parchment lined baking sheet and repeat until you have used all the dough.

3. Take the Mason Jar and dip it into water, then gently press into the dough balls.

4. Bake for 15-18 minutes or until lightly browned.

These are fun and Yummy!

Watch the video of OK B Healthy
making these cookies:
https://www.youtube.com/watch?v=2IWUrZLHgYc&t=335s

2 cups of firmly packed almond flour

1/2 cup of maple syrup

A pinch of salt

Gently mix and roll into balls

Dip the bottom of small Mason Jar into water for each press

Gently press onto ball of dough that has been placed on a cookie sheet

It will look like this

Bake at 350 degrees for 15-18 minutes, let cool

Enjoy!

Marvelous Muffin Mix

1

2 cups of
unbleached flour

2 Tablespoons
sugar

2 teaspoons
baking
powder

1/4 teaspoon
of salt

3

2

1 cup of
milk

1/4 cup
of oil

1 egg,
beaten

1 Combine the dry ingredients and mix together.

2 Combine the wet ingredients in a smaller bowl and mix together.

3 Pour the wet ingredients in the smaller bowl into the dry ingredients in the larger bowl and mix well.

Here is the marvelous part:

After mixing the basic recipe you can add whatever additional flavors that you would like! If you want the whole batch to be one flavor, simply add 1 cup of the filling to the mix. If you want to make individual flavor filled muffins, fill your muffin cup 1/3 of the way with the basic mix, then add no more than 1 Tablespoon of filling on top. Then cover with the mix until the cup is 2/3 filled.

If you choose to add a fruit filling make sure the fruit is well drained before adding as a filling! See the next page for more tips!

4 Bake at 425 degrees for 25 minutes. Let cool 5 minutes before taking out of pan.

43

MUFFIN AND CUPCAKE TIPS:

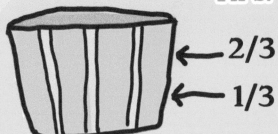

← 2/3
← 1/3

Only fill your muffin cup or paper cupcake liner 2/3 full with batter.

If adding filling individually, fill muffin cup 1/3 full, add your filling, then fill to the 2/3 line with additional batter.

Apples

CHEESE

Pumpkin

Bananas

Cranberries

Blueberries

Ruby often adds a teaspoon of both cinnamon and sugar to her fruit filled muffins. In her cheese muffins she adds some fresh herbs from her garden.

Sweet Streusel Topping:

Added sweetness

1/4 cup of sugar
2 Tablespoons of flour
1/2 teaspoon of cinnamon
1 Tablespoon of softened butter

Mix together and then sprinkle on top of each of the muffins, then bake as directed.

From Farm to Table

SECTION THREE

Local foods from area farms or from your own garden have a shorter time between being harvested and being served at your table. Therefore, it is more likely that all of the nutrition-packed goodness contained in the farm fresh products remains to help fuel your body and keep it strong.

If you want to grow your own, but do not have a suitable space, you can either try container gardening or find a community garden near you.

There are many ways to get local, farm fresh produce even if you cannot grow your own:

Local Farmer's Markets, Farms, and Community Supported Agriculture (CSA) groups in your area can be found at www.localharvest.org.

WHAT IS COMMUNITY SUPPORTED AGRICULTURE?

A system in which a farm operation is supported by shareholders, or members, within the community, who share both the benefits and risks of food production.

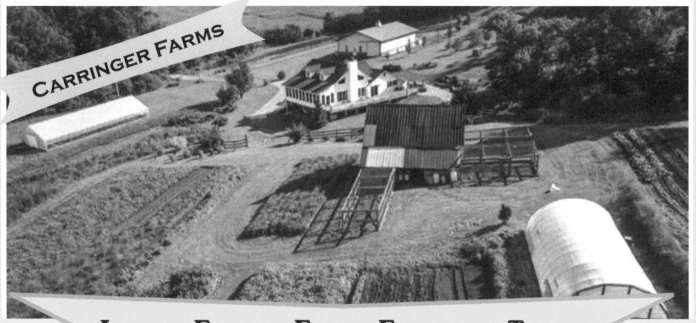

CARRINGER FARMS

LOCAL FOODS: FROM FARM TO TABLE

Don and Belinda Carringer of Carringer Farms (2206 Mountain Grove Road, Franklin, NC) have worked hard to build up their farm to what it is now. Don has been farming all of his life. Don and Belinda sell produce at the Franklin and Swain County Farmer's Markets. They also sell to a few local restaurants.

Belinda specializes in producing jams, jellies and relishes, sourdough bread, potted plants and whipped honey. They also have a large flock of hens and sell their eggs locally. The Carringers are a vital part of making the local foods movement a reality in our area. And they always greet their customers with a smile.

Baked Kale Chips

Ingredients:
1 bunch of kale
1 Tablespoon olive oil
1 teaspoon seasoned salt of your choice

Directions
1. Preheat oven to 350 degrees.
2. With a knife or kitchen shears, carefully remove the leaves from the thick stems and tear into bite-size pieces. Wash and thoroughly dry with a salad spinner or lay on towel to dry. Drizzle kale with olive oil and sprinkle with seasoned salt.
3. Bake until the edges are brown, but not burnt, about 10-15 minutes.
4. Enjoy.

Garlic Parmesan Butternut Squash

Ingredients:
1 lb butternut squash, peeled and cut into small chunks
3 cloves garlic, minced
½ stick butter, melted
Pinch of salt
3 dashes black pepper
Some parsley leaves, finely chopped
⅓ cup grated parmesan cheese

Directions:
1. Preheat oven to 400 degrees.
2. In a salad bowl, toss the butternut squash cubes with the garlic, melted butter, salt, pepper, and parsley leaves.
3. Transfer the butternut squash on a baking sheet. Spread out in an even and single layer, and roast for about 40 minutes, or until the surface becomes light brown and the flesh is tender and soft.
4. Turn off the heat, remove from the oven and sprinkle the Parmesan cheese on top of the squash. Put it back into the oven for 5 minutes until the cheese is melted. Serve immediately.

49

Italian Stuffed Zucchini Boats

Makes 4 Servings

Ingredients:

2 medium zucchini (about 1 ½ pounds), sliced lengthwise
2 Tablespoons olive oil
1 medium onion chopped
1 large garlic clove, minced
1 teaspoon finely chopped fresh marjoram or oregano
2 Tablespoons chopped Italian parsley
1 teaspoon finely grated lemon zest
1 cup cooked rice
¾ cup freshly grated parmesan, divided
Fresh bread crumbs from 1 slice of bread
(generous ½ cup)

Directions:

1. Preheat oven to 350 degrees. Lightly grease a 13x9 baking dish.

2. Hollow out zucchini halves, creating "boats." Finely chop the zucchini flesh and reserve.

3. In a large skillet, heat oil over medium-high heat. Once hot, reduce heat to medium; add the onion and reserved zucchini. Add a little salt and pepper. Sauté for 5 minutes or until onion is translucent and zucchini is softened. Add garlic, herbs and lemon zest. Continue cooking for another minute until fragrant. Remove from heat.

4. Stir in rice and ½ cup parmesan. Adjust seasoning and spoon filling into hollowed out zucchini; place in prepared baking dish.

5. In a small bowl, combine remaining parmesan and fresh bread crumbs. Sprinkle the crumb mixture evenly over the stuffed zucchini. Drizzle with a little olive oil.

6. Bake for 35-45 minutes until topping is golden brown and zucchini is tender.

Annie's Sensational Seasonal Macaroni and Cheese

Start with this base recipe:

Ingredients:

1 pound dried pasta
4 Tablespoons unsalted butter
¼ cup all-purpose flour
2½ cups of whole milk
½ teaspoon mustard
½ teaspoon hot sauce
10 ounces (about 2½ cups) sharp white cheddar cheese, shredded
2 ounces (about ½ cup) white American cheese, shredded
1 teaspoon kosher salt

Directions:

1. Cook pasta according to package directions; drain well.

2. In a large pot, melt butter over medium heat. Whisk in the flour to form a thick paste and cook for 1 minute until bubbly. Whisk in the milk, mustard and hot sauce, cooking until the mixture becomes thickened and bubbly.

3. Take the pot off heat. Gradually add and stir in the white cheddar cheese, white American cheese, and salt to pan. Continue slowly stirring until melted and combined. Add in cooked pasta. Serve immediately.

Adult Supervision needed

Farmer's Market or Garden Fresh Seasonal Additions:

Chop up three cups of seasonal vegetables and sauté in a pan, drizzled with olive oil, over medium heat until softened. Add a pinch of salt and pepper and then stir into your finished mac and cheese.

Summer
corn, green beans, Roma tomatoes, peppers, zucchini

Spring
peas, asparagus, spinach, kale

Autumn
carrots, chard, celery, broccoli

Winter
onions, acorn squash, sweet potatoes

Meat add-ins are great too! Try adding these pre-cooked meats to add another layer of flavor to your Mac-N-Cheese:
Bacon
Ham
Ground Beef
Chicken

Try adding taco seasonings or Italian seasonings to the mix!

Simple and super fresh: Add tomato and avocado slices to the top and serve!

Jonas and Joel's
Golden Armor Juice

Jonas and Joel recommend organic and fresh as possible fruits and veggies to get the full power packed armor their juice provides!

Ingredients:
1 Yellow Bell Pepper
1 Golden Beet
4 Carrots
4 Oranges

Directions:
1. Cut the fruits and vegetables into medium slices that will fit nicely into your juicer or blender.
2. Then put into your juicer or blender and juice it up! This recipe makes 32 ounces, so be prepared with some large glasses. If you are using a blender you will need to sieve the pulp using a mesh strainer.

Shield your immune system with this nutritional juice!

https://www.facebook.com/okbhealthy/videos/2016048535110634/

OK B Healthy
Making Healthy Choices
by Jacqueline Bourne

God made each of us unique in our own way. How boring would life be if we were all exactly the same? God's vast creation has so many varieties of plants, animals, colors and seasons. He made many different foods for us to enjoy; foods that support our growing bodies. He loves us so much!

Man's processed foods may seem convenient, but naturally grown, fresh produce was designed by our Heavenly Father to keep our bodies strong and healthy and full of energy. Even small, gradual changes in the food we eat can make a difference. Why not give it a try?
My family has made many changes in our food choices and we love it! In fact, right now, we are doing a fun experiment and are eliminating all processed sugars from the food we eat for one full year. We have been doing it for five months and we feel so much better!

 I would suggest that you look for fun ways to alter your family's favorite recipes to make them healthier. Choosing fresh, nutritious foods with real ingredients that are rich in vitamins and minerals will help supply the energy your family needs to "go and grow". I have put together a list of healthy substitutions to share with you, (on page 56) that have helped my family and me in our quest to live a healthier lifestyle.

Follow OK B Healthy on Youtube, Facebook, and Instagram to learn more about healthy eating and living. You will find great recipes and amazing advice.

Healthy Alternatives and Substitutions

Brought to you by: OK B Healthy, Jacqueline Bourne

When substituting ingredients in a recipe, you have to become like a scientist and experiment. Typically it is a 1:1 ratio, which means, that if for instance, a recipe calls for 1 cup of oil then you would instead add 1 cup of applesauce. Each recipe is different, so you may need to adjust. Try the 1:1 and see what you think, then add more or less until you get the proportion that fits your taste!

INSTEAD OF: TRY THIS:

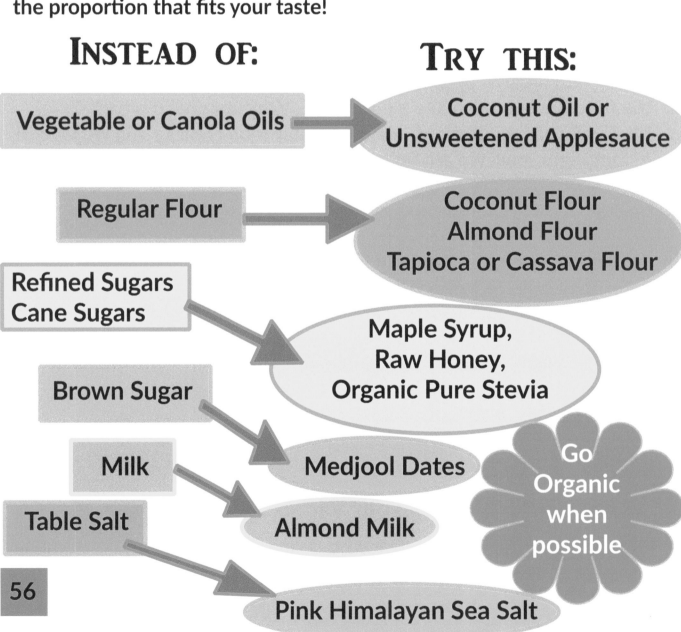

Vegetable or Canola Oils → Coconut Oil or Unsweetened Applesauce

Regular Flour → Coconut Flour / Almond Flour / Tapioca or Cassava Flour

Refined Sugars / Cane Sugars → Maple Syrup, Raw Honey, Organic Pure Stevia

Brown Sugar → Medjool Dates

Milk → Almond Milk

Table Salt → Pink Himalayan Sea Salt

Go Organic when possible

Fun with Garnishes

We have learned about food presentation on page 6. Now let us look at three simple ways to garnish your plate and fancy it up! It is very important to remember your knife safety skills and to concentrate on using proper knife technique when working on these garnishes.

The first step is to thoroughly wash and dry your carrot, lemon, or radishes.

First peel off the top layer of carrot. Then grate the carrot into thin strips. They will naturally curl.

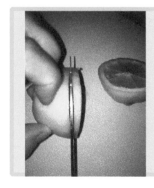  

Cut a thin slice of lemon. Cut a slit a little more than half way through. Pick up and twist.

Make sure the radish is dry, as it can be slippery when wet. Cut the root and top off of the radish. Cut slices, making sure to stop before cutting all the way through. Throw in ice water after cutting. When ready to plate, thoroughly dry the radish .

Parent Tips:
Fun with Fruits and Veggies

1. Make a game out of preparing and eating new foods

<u>Choose to Chop Salad</u> – These are fun to make as a family because there is a job for every age. Everyone can pick what kind of fruits or veggies they want to add in. Older children can help peel and chop, and younger children can help add all of the ingredients and toss them together with a dressing (honey works great on fruit, or ranch on vegetables). Try to add different textures in: canned mandarin oranges, wild rice, pickled beets, crispy wonton noodles, a crumbly cheese, or toasted nuts can turn a boring salad into a tasty treat.

<u>New Taste Treasure Hunt</u>- Try new fruits or vegetables with a friend or family and call it a Treasure Hunt! While grocery shopping in the produce section, have everyone find a fruit or vegetable they have never tasted before. Then when you return home, wash and cut into bite size pieces. Have everyone try a couple of bites and talk about what it tastes like. Is it sweet or spicy? Sour or salty? Does it taste like anything else you have eaten before? What would it be fun to eat with? You could even have the children make up a chart to journal their reaction to each of the new items.

2. Fix foods in a new and interesting way

Cowboy Dinner – Campfires are a great opportunity to slice up some veggies, put them in the middle of a square of foil, and sprinkle with some olive oil, salt, and pepper (or marinade of choice). Fold up and crimp the edges of the foil to make an enclosed packet and pop the packet on a fire grate, or on the coals of the fire. The veggies are done when the pocket is bendable or soft to the touch. Enjoy with a good yodel like the cowboys of yore.

Fruit or Vegetable Kabobs – Cut fruit or veggies and cheese into cubes and put them onto kabob sticks in different combinations. Have ranch dressing to dip veggies into and vanilla yogurt for the fruit. Be aware that younger children may need some instructions on safe handling of the kabob sticks.

Cold Treat Delights- Freezing grapes, making smoothies, cutting fruits into shapes with cookie cutters, and making popsicles are great ways to introduce more fruits into your child's diet and, will most likely, have them asking for more!

Flavor is a social Cooking Club that meets at Macon Appliance in Franklin, North Carolina. It is a modern potluck where you chose your dish to share from the monthly chosen cookbook. New flavors and fresh cooking techniques and methods are shared. Everyone is welcome!

Flavor meets the 3rd Monday of the month at 6:30 p.m. The club also hosts quarterly special events. Check out their Facebook page for more information.

www.facebook.com/flavorcookbookclub/

Suminski Family Books is a member in good standing with:

www.suminskifamilybooks.com